I0814215

Still Learning You

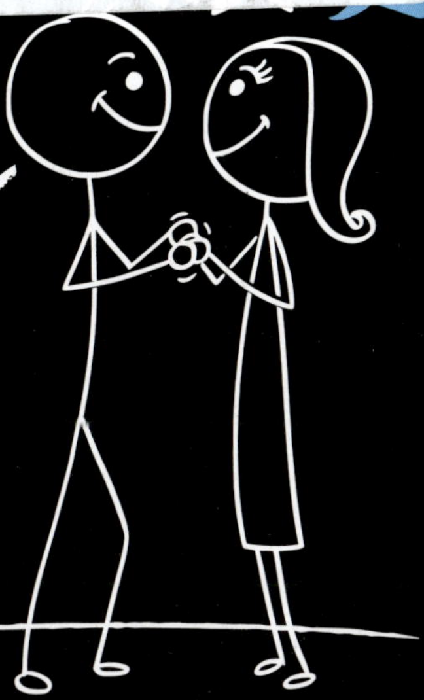

DATE-NIGHT QUESTIONS FOR EVERY STAGE OF MARRIAGE

CHAD & MARIANNE HOWARD

© 2026 Chad & Marianne Howard

All Scripture quotations are from The Holy Bible, English Standard Version® (ESV®), Text Edition: 2016, copyright © 2001 by Crossway Bible, a publishing ministry of Good News Publishers. Used by permission. All rights reserved.

All rights reserved. No part of this publication may be reproduced, stored in a retrieval system, or transmitted in any form or by any means—electronic, mechanical, photocopy, recording, or any other means—except for brief quotation in critical reviews, without the prior permission of the publisher.

Published by D6 Family Ministry
114 Bush Road
Nashville, TN 37217
d6family.com

ISBN: 9781614842163
Printed in the United States of America

CURIOSITY, CONNECTION, AND A TISSUE BOX

Before smartphones, apps, or AI, we sat at a weathered picnic table with a tissue box, yes, a real tissue box we emptied out on purpose, filled with scraps of paper and curiosity.

We were newly married, and someone gave us a challenge that changed everything: "A strong marriage is built by two people who keep learning about each other on purpose, for a lifetime." In other words, become a student of your spouse. Stay curious. Take notes. Ask good questions. Because people don't stay the same, and neither should the way we love them. So we got to work by writing ten questions each, folding them up, and dropping them into that little makeshift box.

What happened next surprised us. With every question we pulled, another layer of who we were and who we were becoming came to light. We found ourselves laughing, pausing, and even tearing up at times. We were doing more than swapping answers; we were building trust, intimacy, and connection, one honest conversation at a time.

That day started a tradition that's lasted decades: intentionally pursuing each other's hearts again and again, in every season.

This booklet is an invitation into that same pursuit. The questions inside have helped us laugh more, listen better, and love deeper. We hope they'll do the same for you and help you create moments that draw you closer than ever before.

Chad & Marianne Howard

INTRO

Whether you've been married for two months or two decades, this little book is for you. It's not about having the perfect relationship; it's about creating space for intentional connection, honest conversation, and the kind of love that keeps growing, no matter what season you're in.

Each page is built on the truth of Scripture, because love doesn't grow from good intentions alone. Marriage isn't just a contract; it's a covenant (promise) before God, designed to reflect His faithful, never-ending love. It's grounded in grace, strengthened by forgiveness, and sustained by the hope we find in Jesus and the love He has demonstrated for us.

HOW TO USE THIS BOOKLET

Each page includes a simple, heartfelt question on the left side; something to cultivate emotional intimacy and understanding. On the right, you'll find a short devotional thought and a verse from Scripture, thoughtfully paired to speak into that topic.

There's no right way to go through this. You might use one page a week over dinner. Or flip through and pick the one that fits your current season. You can answer the questions in a journal or simply discuss them on a date night, during a walk, or a late-night couch conversation.

But here's the heart behind it: Marriage gets stronger when we pause to see each other not just in the big, sweeping milestones, but in the quiet questions and the daily "I'm still choosing you" moments. So go slow. Be honest. Laugh a lot. Cry if you need to. Pray together.

Let this be more than a book. Let it be a doorway into deeper connection, deeper faith, and deeper love. You've got something special here, and it's worth the investment.

IF WE HAD TO SWITCH LIVES FOR A DAY, WHAT'S THE FIRST THING YOU'D DO AS ME?

"Let all that you do be done in love."

1 CORINTHIANS 16:14

DEVOTIONAL THOUGHT:

Empathy is the gateway to compassion, and few questions build empathy like imagining life through your spouse's eyes. When you trade places in your mind, you start to notice things you may have missed: the pressure they carry, the invisible tasks they juggle, the hopes they quietly hold. Marriage grows when we shift from thinking, "Why do they do it that way?" to "What must it feel like to carry that?"

This kind of understanding doesn't just change your conversations, it changes your reactions. You soften. You serve. You choose grace.

Jesus chose to walk among us in human flesh and experience our limitations, frailty, and burdens. When we do the same for each other, even in playful questions like this one, we mirror His love in the most intentional way.

WHAT'S THE WEIRDEST OR MOST UNNECESSARY THING WE'VE EVER IMPULSE-BOUGHT?

"A joyful heart is good medicine, but a crushed spirit dries up the bones."

PROVERBS 17:22

DEVOTIONAL THOUGHT:

Laughter is glue. It bonds you in ways that serious conversations can't. It's in the shared smirks over inside jokes, the laughter that erupts at midnight over something ridiculous, the moments when everything goes wrong, but at least you're together. Don't overlook these silly memories. They're a gift in their own way. They remind you that joy belongs in the heart of your marriage.

Marriage isn't just about deep talks and big dreams; it's also about finding delight in everyday moments and not taking yourselves too seriously. So laugh today. Reminisce about that ridiculous purchase. Let joy remind you: this journey is better because you're walking it side by side, together.

WHAT'S ONE THING I DO THAT MAKES YOU FEEL TRULY LOVED AND VALUED?

> **"Love one another with brotherly affection. Outdo one another in showing honor."**
>
> ROMANS 12:10

DEVOTIONAL THOUGHT:

The world teaches us to win, to achieve, to be first. But what if the goal in marriage was to *outdo one another in love?* Not in competition, but in compassion. Not in being right, but in being kind. When you take the time to ask, "What makes you feel loved?" you're doing more than listening; you're inviting your spouse to be fully seen. When you act on their answer, you're strengthening the kind of trust that deepens over time. Small, consistent gestures matter: a text at lunch, a quiet hug at the door, doing that one thing they dread without being asked.

Marriage deepens when we stop assuming and start asking. When we honor each other with intentional love, we reflect the heart of Jesus, who sees, serves, and never stops pursuing us.

HOW CAN I PRAY FOR YOU IN A WAY THAT TRULY MEETS YOUR NEEDS IN THIS SEASON?

"Therefore, confess your sins to one another and pray for one another, that you may be healed. The prayer of a righteous person has great power as it is working."

JAMES 5:16

DEVOTIONAL THOUGHT:

Prayer isn't just something we do for each other; it's something that binds our hearts to each other. Asking, "How can I pray for you?" may sound simple, but it opens the door to the places in our hearts that feel fragile, unseen, or heavy. It's a gentle invitation to be known without judgment. When we bring those burdens before God together, healing begins—not just in the situation, but in our connection. Walls come down. Tenderness rises.

Don't stop there, take a moment to pray for your spouse out loud, speaking their name and their needs before God.

When you remember that request a day or a week later? It tells your spouse, "You matter. Your soul matters." Let prayer become more than a routine. Let it be the tether that binds you through hope, hardship, and healing—holding your hearts together as God shapes your story.

WHAT'S ONE FEAR OR INSECURITY YOU HAVE THAT I MAY NOT BE AWARE OF?

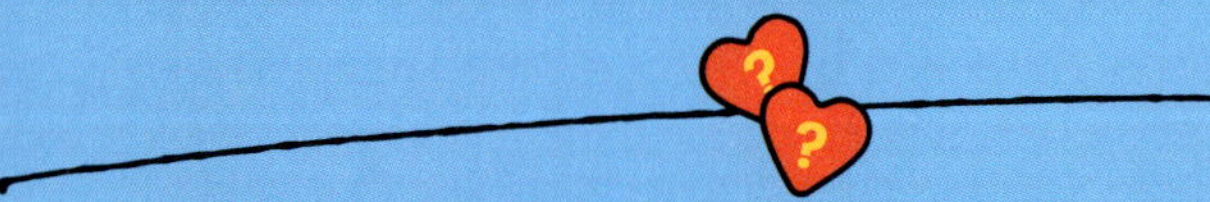

> **"Let each of you look not only to his own interests, but also to the interests of others."**
>
> PHILIPPIANS 2:4

DEVOTIONAL THOUGHT:

It's easy to love the parts of our spouse we see. But real intimacy grows when we care about the fears we *don't* see, when we lean in instead of shutting down.

Asking this question is brave. Answering it is courageous. When done in love, it becomes sacred ground. Marriage isn't just about solving problems; it's about creating a safe space for honesty and transparency. Your spouse may not need a solution today. They may just need to be believed, held, or heard. When you listen without trying to fix, you communicate: "You don't have to be perfect to be loved here." That kind of love? It casts out fear. So slow down. Ask the question. Let their answer deepen your connection in ways you didn't expect.

WHAT'S ONE HABIT OR SMALL CHANGE I COULD MAKE THAT WOULD IMPROVE OUR MARRIAGE?

> **"Whoever walks with the wise becomes wise, but the companion of fools will suffer harm."**
>
> PROVERBS 13:20

DEVOTIONAL THOUGHT:

It takes courage to ask this question. But small changes, made in love, are the seeds of transformation. The healthiest marriages aren't made of grand gestures. They're built one quiet decision at a time, choosing to listen, to adjust, to grow. When you invite your spouse to speak into your blind spots, you're not admitting failure; you're demonstrating the humility that values the relationship more than yourself. Seeking this kind of wisdom shows your spouse that you desire to be more like Jesus and that you need their help. This kind of growth isn't weakness; it's worship.

Even one small change, such as maintaining more eye contact, reducing distractions, or speaking a kind word before sleep, can breathe fresh life into your connection. Ask the question. Listen with open hands. Thank God that marriage is a place where iron sharpens iron, and love keeps showing up, day by day.

WHAT'S A CHALLENGE WE'VE OVERCOME TOGETHER THAT MADE US STRONGER?

> **"Not only that, but we rejoice in our sufferings, knowing that suffering produces endurance, and endurance produces character, and character produces hope."**
>
> ROMANS 5:3–4

Some of your deepest strength was forged in your hardest seasons. Strength doesn't come despite the struggle; it comes through it. You didn't ask for the challenge, but you faced it together. Somewhere in the grit and grace of that season, your love got tougher. Truer. Tested and found unshakable. This kind of resilience isn't accidental; it's the result of walking hand-in-hand through storms with Christ at the center. When you reflect on what you've overcome, you're not just remembering pain; you're remembering *provision.* Celebrate that. Tell the story again. Let it remind you: God has carried you before, and He'll do it again.

Marriage isn't the absence of hardship. It's the presence of faithfulness.

And your story? It's living proof that love rooted in Christ doesn't just survive, it grows stronger.

WHAT'S ONE THING WE COULD BE DOING BETTER TO MODEL A STRONG FAITH FOR OUR FAMILY?

> **"Be imitators of me, as I am of Christ."**
>
> 1 CORINTHIANS 11:1

DEVOTIONAL THOUGHT:

Your kids won't remember every devotional you led, but they'll never forget watching your faith in action. They'll see how you spoke to each other when no one was watching. How you prayed when things felt uncertain. How you kept showing up for each other with grace and determination. Modeling faith isn't about perfection; it's about direction.

It's in the way you live your "yes" to Jesus when life is full and when it's frustrating. It's how you choose Scripture over sarcasm, presence over distraction, and humility over having the last word. So take inventory, not of what you're doing wrong, but of what you could do more intentionally. Because when your marriage quietly reflects Christ, your family notices.

And the faith they see in you? It may just become the faith they carry forward.

IF YOU COULD GO BACK IN TIME AND GIVE YOURSELF ONE PIECE OF RELATIONSHIP ADVICE BEFORE WE GOT MARRIED, WHAT WOULD IT BE?

"Let all bitterness and wrath and anger and clamor and slander be put away from you... Be kind to one another, tenderhearted, forgiving one another, as God in Christ forgave you."

EPHESIANS 4:31–32

DEVOTIONAL THOUGHT:

If you could sit across from your newly engaged selves, starry-eyed and full of big dreams, you'd probably smile and then offer a little wisdom earned from the road behind.

You've learned that love isn't always loud; it's built on kindness in the chaos. On forgiving quickly and choosing humility when pride feels easier. On soft answers instead of sharp comebacks. If you could go back, maybe you'd say: "It's not about being right. It's about being gentle with each other's hearts."

But here's the beauty: you *can* go forward with that wisdom now. Every day is another chance to lead with compassion, to listen more than defend, and to love like you've learned something. God's grace has carried you this far, and it's still teaching you how to love well.

(HUSBANDS, THIS ONE'S FOR YOU.
START WITH THIS QUESTION AND KEEP LISTENING.)

WHAT'S ONE WAY I CAN LEAD OUR MARRIAGE WITH MORE LOVE AND LEADERSHIP?

> **"Husbands, love your wives, as Christ loved the church and gave himself up for her."**
>
> EPHESIANS 5:25

DEVOTIONAL THOUGHT:

Leadership in marriage isn't about control; it's about care. It means laying your life down. Jesus redefined leadership, not with demands, but with a towel and a basin. He served. He sacrificed. He led with strength wrapped in gentleness.

Loving leadership starts with tuning your heart to hers. It's choosing patience over pride. It's listening when you'd rather fix. It's stepping in when things get hard, not to take control, but to love with courage and humility.

You won't always get it right. But when your heart is yielded to Jesus, love leads the way. Because every time you lead with love instead of ego, you reflect the One who loved you first. That kind of leadership? It builds trust. It brings peace. It sets the tone for a marriage that honors Jesus and blesses your home.

(WIVES, THIS ONE'S FOR YOU.
START WITH THIS QUESTION AND KEEP LISTENING.)

WHAT'S ONE WAY I CAN SHOW YOU THAT I ADMIRE AND RESPECT YOU MORE INTENTIONALLY?

"Let the wife see that she respects her husband."

EPHESIANS 5:33B

DEVOTIONAL THOUGHT:

Respect isn't about superiority; it's about value. When you speak words of admiration, when you notice his efforts, when you choose to trust his heart even in weakness, you aren't just building his confidence. You're building your marriage. A man who feels respected by his wife often finds the courage to lead, serve, and love with greater intention and determination.

This doesn't mean agreeing on everything. It means assuming the best. It means asking questions instead of accusing motives. It means cheering louder than the world criticizes. Most of all, it means remembering that your respect isn't based on his perfection, but reflects your love for Christ and your commitment to honor the one you chose.

HOW HAVE YOU SEEN GOD WORKING IN OUR MARRIAGE LATELY?

"Behold, I am doing a new thing;
now it springs forth, do you not perceive it?"

ISAIAH 43:19A

DEVOTIONAL THOUGHT:

Sometimes, we miss God's work because we're looking for fireworks instead of faithfulness. But often, His hand shows up in the slow healing of an old wound, the quiet unity in a hard conversation, or the peace that makes no sense except for His presence. When you pause to reflect on how God is moving in your marriage, right now, you begin to notice that grace has been growing, even when life felt stuck.

God doesn't just fix what's broken. He makes *new things* out of what feels forgotten.

So stop and celebrate what He's doing, even if it feels small. The very act of noticing might be the start of something even greater.

WHAT'S SOMETHING I MISSED HEARING FROM YOU THAT YOU WISH I HAD TAKEN TIME TO UNDERSTAND?

“A fool takes no pleasure in understanding, but only in expressing his opinion.”

PROVERBS 18:2

DEVOTIONAL THOUGHT:

Listening is more than staying quiet while your spouse talks. It’s about valuing understanding over being right. In marriage, it’s easy to slip into defense mode and interrupt, assume, or push your point a little harder. But love doesn’t just speak, it listens. It leans in. It says, “I want to understand your heart, not just hear your words.”

True wisdom begins when we stop trying to win and start trying to understand. That kind of listening builds trust. It softens conflict. It reflects a love marked by grace and wisdom.

For husbands and wives, this means making space for emotion, for story, for silence. It means resisting the urge to fix and instead offering presence. It’s listening not just to the words spoken, but to what’s underneath them. When you seek to understand your spouse, you gain more than insight; you gain connection.

Jesus listens to us like that: fully, patiently, without interruption. It may feel small, but listening to understand is one of the most powerful ways to reflect Christ in your marriage.

WHAT'S ONE SMALL, EVERYDAY THING I DO THAT MAKES YOU SMILE?

"The light of the eyes rejoices the heart, and good news refreshes the bones."

PROVERBS 15:30

DEVOTIONAL THOUGHT:

It's easy to think love is made in grand moments, but often, it's found in the little things.

It's the little things, isn't it? The shared inside joke. The way they make your coffee just right. That wink across the room. The way you still reach for their hand after all these years. The glance that says, "I see you, and I love you."

God uses the smallest gestures to remind us of the biggest truths. God designed love not just for mountaintop moments, but for laundry days, school pick-ups, and grocery runs. He uses everyday gestures, like nudging a particular verse in our mind when we need it or putting a wise friend in our path to help us. These everyday, providential gestures remind us we're seen, valued, and loved deeply.

Celebrate these simple moments today. Notice them. Name them. Let your spouse hear how their small gestures bring joy to your heart. Because in these tiny, daily details, we experience a love that refreshes the soul, brings joy to our hearts, and reminds us of God's delight in the ordinary moments of life together.

IF YOU COULD MASTER ONE RANDOM SKILL INSTANTLY, WHAT WOULD IT BE?

> **"So, whether you eat or drink, or whatever you do, do all to the glory of God."**
>
> 1 CORINTHIANS 10:31

DEVOTIONAL THOUGHT:

This question may seem lighthearted, but it reveals something powerful: what inspires you, what excites you, what lights you up. God wired your spouse with passions for a reason. When you take time to delight in what delights them, even silly or unexpected things, you affirm their uniqueness. In marriage, part of the adventure is learning to cheer for each other's dreams—even the random ones. Love says, "If it matters to you, it matters to me." That kind of support, whether it's for learning to play the banjo or fixing up an old truck, deepens connection in beautiful ways.

HOW CAN I SUPPORT YOU BETTER IN THE DAILY STRESS AND PRESSURES OF LIFE?

"Bear one another's burdens, and so fulfill the law of Christ."

GALATIANS 6:2

DEVOTIONAL THOUGHT:

Marriage isn't always a fairytale; it's a tag-team. Some days, one of you is running the race while the other hands off the water, cheering from the sidelines. Other days, you're both hurdling through the chaos, high-fiving between laundry loads and late-night talks.

Galatians 6:2 calls us to carry each other's burdens, not just emotionally, but practically too. Let your love be a safe landing after a hard day. Fold their shirt. Pray over their inbox. Ask, "What can I take off your plate today?"

Love looks like asking, serving, folding, praying, and doing it again tomorrow.

IF WE COULD TAKE A SPONTANEOUS TRIP ANYWHERE IN THE WORLD TOMORROW, WHERE WOULD WE GO?

> **"The heart of man plans his way, but the Lord establishes his steps."**
>
> PROVERBS 16:9

DEVOTIONAL THOUGHT:

Where would we go if we could leave tomorrow? It's more than a travel question; it's an invitation to dream again. Maybe it's a beach vacation, a cabin in the mountains, or your favorite coffee shop across town with no agenda. The destination doesn't matter as much as the desire behind it: *adventure, connection, and rest.* Dreaming together reconnects you to purpose and reminds you that life is more than calendars and soccer practice.

Proverbs 16:9 reminds us that while we plan, *God directs.* So instead of holding your dreams with tight fists, hold them like an open map, ready for detours, divine reroutes, and beautiful surprises.

Dream freely. Plan playfully. Trust fully. Your love story was never meant to stay in one place.

WHAT'S ONE THING I DO THAT UNINTENTIONALLY HURTS YOU, AND HOW CAN I CHANGE THAT?

> **"Let every person be quick to hear, slow to speak, slow to anger."**
>
> JAMES 1:19

DEVOTIONAL THOUGHT:

Every marriage has blind spots, little things that sting more than we realize. A rushed reply. A poorly timed joke. A habit that brushes past their heart. We don't mean to hurt each other, but *unintentional doesn't mean unimpactful.*

That's why this question matters. It isn't just deep; it's intentional. It says, *"I love you enough to ask. I trust you enough to tell me."*

James 1:19 is a roadmap for this kind of love: *Listen fast. Talk slow. Stay calm.* When we lead with humility and receive feedback with grace, something amazing happens: walls fall, understanding grows, and hurt begins to heal. This isn't about shame; it's about growth. You're not failing; you're fine-tuning. You're learning to love with intention.

IF WE COULD OUTSOURCE ONE HOUSEHOLD CHORE FOREVER, WHAT WOULD IT BE, AND WHAT WOULD WE DO WITH THE EXTRA TIME?

"Whatever you do, work heartily, as for the Lord and not for men."

COLOSSIANS 3:23

DEVOTIONAL THOUGHT:

It turns out, "whatever you do" includes the stuff no one wants to do. Sometimes it looks like unclogging a drain, scraping week-old spaghetti off a plate, or folding yet another mountain of laundry that mysteriously regenerates overnight.

But here's the thing: love often shows up in the mundane stuff. Shared responsibility is a quiet, powerful form of love. When you split the grocery run, tackle the dishes without being asked, or take one for the team by dealing with the mystery smell in the fridge, you're not just keeping a house running. You're keeping your marriage strong.

Marriage isn't a chore chart; it's a partnership. One where small acts of service become declarations of love. Sure, go ahead and dream about outsourcing the bathroom cleaning. But in the meantime, serve each other with joy... and maybe rubber gloves. Because every time you choose humility over resentment, service over sarcasm, and shared laughter over silent frustration, you're making the choice to work heartily, as if Jesus Himself asked you to do it.

WHAT'S A SILLY HABIT OR QUIRK OF MINE THAT YOU SECRETLY (OR NOT-SO-SECRETLY) LOVE?

> **"Put on then, as God's chosen ones, holy and beloved, compassionate hearts, kindness, humility, meekness, and patience, bearing with one another and, if one has a complaint against another, forgiving each other; as the Lord has forgiven you, so you also must forgive."**
>
> COLOSSIANS 3:12–13

DEVOTIONAL THOUGHT:

In marriage, quirks are inevitable. Sometimes they drive you crazy, and sometimes they endear your spouse even more deeply to you. Choosing grace in the face of quirks, annoyances, and imperfections reflects the patience and kindness of God toward us.

Graciousness doesn't erase quirks; it covers them with affection. It laughs gently when socks miss the laundry basket and smiles lovingly at quirky habits that others might find puzzling. When grace flavors your words and interactions, your marriage grows sweeter, richer, and more deeply connected. Just as God continually showers you with grace, extend that grace generously to each other, turning your unique quirks into beloved reminders of the beautiful partnership you share.

WHERE IN OUR MARRIAGE DO WE NEED TO INVITE JESUS TO HOLD THINGS TOGETHER, INSTEAD OF TRYING TO CONTROL IT OURSELVES?

"And he is before all things, and in him all things hold together."

COLOSSIANS 1:17

DEVOTIONAL THOUGHT:

"In him all things hold together." That's not just a verse for creation, it's a promise for your marriage. When life feels scattered by busyness, misunderstandings, or unmet expectations, it's tempting to grip tighter, to manage on your own. But holding things together is not your job. It's God's.

Jesus doesn't stand apart from your relationship; He goes before you and upholds you in every season: joyful, ordinary, or difficult. The real question is whether you'll trust Him with the places that feel fragile.

What happens if you stop striving to fix everything and instead surrender your need to control? What if you prayed together: "Jesus, hold this for us. Carry what we can't. Be the center again."

Your strength as a couple isn't found in perfect effort, but in Christ's steady presence. He is not just holding the world together, He's holding you together. Let Him.

WHAT'S ONE THING WE WANT TO BE KNOWN FOR AS A COUPLE?

> **"By this all people will know that you are my disciples, if you have love for one another."**
>
> JOHN 13:35

DEVOTIONAL THOUGHT:

Your love tells a story to your kids, your friends, your family, and even strangers watching from the sidelines. Whether you realize it or not, the way you speak, serve, sacrifice, and support each other is a living message. So the real question is: *What do you want it to say?*

A couple who forgave quickly?

Who prayed in the chaos and danced in the kitchen?

Who weathered storms with steady grace or just held on tighter when life got heavy?

That kind of love is powerful. Not perfect, but *profound*. Because it points to something greater than chemistry or compatibility, it points to Christ.

You don't need a platform to testify. Your marriage preaches. From the grocery runs to the hard conversations, people are watching, and what they see can spark hope.

So, today, take one small step to love louder, deeper, and more deliberately. Live in such a way that when people see your love, they pause and think, "Whatever they have, I want it. I wonder if it's Jesus."

WHAT ARE YOU MOST GRATEFUL FOR IN OUR MARRIAGE, AND HOW CAN WE KEEP GROWING FROM HERE?

> **"I thank my God in all my remembrance of you… because of your partnership in the gospel from the first day until now."**
>
> PHILIPPIANS 1:3, 5

Every love story has chapters of joy and pages of pain, but the beauty of yours is in the *partnership*. You've laughed. You've fought. You've whispered prayers and held each other through storms. And you're still here, still choosing each other, still building something that lasts. Gratitude is the heartbeat of lasting love. It reminds you where you've been. It strengthens your "yes" for the road ahead.

Take time to look back, but don't stop there. Ask God for fresh vision, deeper connection, and new ways to serve each other and His kingdom together. Because your marriage isn't just a gift, it's a testimony. Your best chapters, with Christ at the center, are still being written.

HOW HAS GOD'S GOODNESS SURPRISED US OVER THE YEARS, EVEN IN HARD SEASONS?

"Surely goodness and mercy shall follow me all the days of my life..."

PSALM 23:6A

DEVOTIONAL THOUGHT:

Sometimes God's goodness is loud: answered prayers, big breakthroughs, and wide-open doors. But more often, it's quiet. Subtle. The kind that shows up like a whisper in the middle of a storm. A sliver of peace in chaos. A gentle nudge toward each other when life is pulling you apart.

Looking back, you may not have seen His hand in the moment, but you can see the fingerprints now. The way He sustained you when you were worn thin. The way He softened your hearts when they could've gone cold. The way He used disappointment not to defeat you, but to deepen your love.

God's goodness isn't just something that visits you on mountaintops. It follows you. Pursues you. Even into the valleys...especially into the valleys.

So don't miss the miracle hidden in the mess. The laughter that returned after a hard conversation. The unexpected provision when you were running on empty. The closeness that came from clinging to each other and to Him. Because sometimes the greatest surprise is realizing that even in your lowest moments, goodness and mercy never left your side.

HOW CAN WE BE MORE INTENTIONAL ABOUT MAKING OUR MARRIAGE A PRIORITY, EVEN IN THE MIDDLE OF BUSY SEASONS?

"Look carefully then how you walk, not as unwise but as wise, making the best use of the time..."

EPHESIANS 5:15–16A

DEVOTIONAL THOUGHT:

Let's be honest: "We're just in a busy season" often becomes a permission slip to neglect connection.

But here's the hard truth: when we blame disconnection on busyness, we're saying our schedule matters more than our marriage. Marriage doesn't pause when life picks up. Ephesians says to walk *wisely* and *make the best use of time.* That means love doesn't get leftovers; it deserves strategy. Busy seasons shouldn't weaken your marriage; they should reveal its strength.

So plan with purpose:

- Schedule a 15-minute daily check-in (yes, on the calendar).
- Put a weekly "us" date on the calendar (even if it's just a coffee run).
- Write down something you appreciate about your spouse and leave it somewhere unexpected.
- Share your calendars weekly, so you can intentionally support each other.
- Choose one chore your spouse dislikes and handle it quietly.
- Plan a tech-free hour each evening, fully present and focused.
- Make a habit of asking, "How can I help today?" (Then actually do it).
- Take a ten-minute walk together after dinner, phones off, connection on.
- Make bedtime "thank you" time, naming one thing your spouse did that day.
- Create a signal or code word meaning, "I need a quick moment with you," ensuring immediate emotional connection.

Connection doesn't come from extra time. It comes from intentional time. Your love is worth more than survival mode. Protect it. Pursue it. Build your calendar around what you value most.